ICE AGE 3
DAWN OF THE DINOSAURS

Facts and Fun

Dawn of the Dinosaurs TM and © 2008 Twentieth Century Fox Film Corporation. All Rights Reserved.

First published in the UK by HarperCollins Children's Books in 2009

1 3 5 7 9 10 8 6 4 2

ISBN-13: 978-0-00-784-735-8

www.harpercollins.co.uk

SiD FaCt FiLe

WHAT IS HE? A giant sloth.
PLACE IN THE HERD: The lovable
goofball.
LIKES: Sleeping. Sid could sleep
all day, and often does!
DISLIKES: Having to give up
the dinosaur babies when
Momma Dino comes
looking for them.

DIEGO'S RESCUE

Ellie is stuck on a cliff. Help Diego jump up the ledges to rescue her. Ledges with an odd number on them will crumble if he lands on them. Only ledges with an even number on them are safe. Draw the route Diego should take.

FINISH

17

20

22

25

18

19

16

11

14

9

12

10

5

3

8

6

1

7

4

2

START

CRESS DiNO CRESTS

You will need:
Clean empty eggshells
Empty egg box
Cotton wool balls
Cress seeds
Water
Paints and paint brushes
A grown-up to help

1 Cut the cups from the bottom of the egg box to make shallow dishes for your dinosaur eggs to sit in, or use an egg cup.

2 Paint dinosaur faces on the eggshells and leave them to dry.

3 Dampen cotton wool balls with water and place one in the bottom of each of your dinosaur eggs.

4 Sprinkle a layer of cress seeds in each one and place them on a window ledge.

5 Sprinkle with a little water each day and watch your cress dinosaur crests grow!

HOME IS WHERE THE HERD IS

Draw your own family below.

A herd is a family or group of animals that all look out for each other and stick together. Manny, Ellie, Sid, Diego, Crash and Eddie are a herd, even though they are all different kinds of animals.

MANNY AND ELLIE FACT FILE

WHAT ARE THEY? Mammoths.
PLACE IN THE HERD: Manny and Ellie are the heads of the herd and
are about to have a baby mammoth.
LIKES: Getting everything ready for
their new baby.
DISLIKES: Feeling small in the
jungle world when they meet
dinosaurs for the first time.

Scrat's Scavenger Hunt

Scrat spends all his time searching for nuts, but there are lots of other things you could find on a scavenger hunt at home and in the garden. Find a friend and see who can find all the things on Scrat's list first.

A button
A leaf
A round stone
A pencil
A flower
A book
A twig

SiD'S SQUARES

Find a friend to play this game with. Take turns joining up two dots in the grid below. The aim of the game is to complete as many squares as possible. Each time you complete a square, write your initials inside it. Score one point for each completed square and two points if the square contains a dinosaur egg. The winner is the player with the most points.

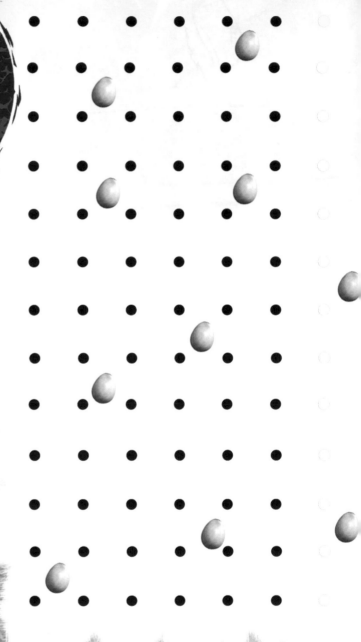

DIEGO FACT FILE

WHAT IS HE?
A sabre-toothed tiger.
PLACE IN THE HERD:
Just a lovable
kitty-cat, even
though he should
be a dangerous
predator!
LIKES: Running.
DISLIKES: That
he's not as
fast as he
used to be.

HOW MANY MANNYS?

How many pictures of Manny can you count here? Be careful, some of them may be Ellie!

WHAT HAPPENED?

Complete the story opposite by choosing words from the list below!

Buck

Dinosaurs

Falls

Piranhas

Herd

Three

Pineapple

Manny

Weasel

Fight

Peaches

OX

Babies

Plants

Momma

Aardvark

Broccoli

Rudy

Diego and Sid felt left out because _____ and Ellie were going to have a baby. They were worried they would no longer be part of the ____. Diego left by himself. Sid found _____ dinosaur eggs and decided to keep them. But there was a problem: the dino babies' _____ came to find them, and took Sid with them to Lava _____, in the land beneath the Ice Age where the other dinosaurs live.

The others followed to rescue him. On the way, they met Buck, an adventuring _____, who helped them when they almost got eaten by strange _____ and fierce _____. Buck was trying to find a dinosaur called ____, who he once had a _____ with.

Eventually, they found Sid, who realised that the dino _____ would be happier with the other dinosaurs, because they were now too big for him to look after. They made their way home, but not before Ellie had a baby called _____. ____ decided to stay in the dino world, to continue his battle with Rudy.

scrat and scratte fact file

WHAT ARE THEY? Sabre-toothed squirrels.

PLACE IN THE HERD: Scrat and Scratte tag along in the hope that the herd might lead them to some nuts.

LIKES: Nuts.

DISLIKES: Not having any nuts.

POSTCARD FROM BUCK

Buck decided to stay behind in the land of the dinosaurs
when his new friends went back to the Ice Age. Ask an adult to
help you cut out this postcard, then write a message from
Buck to his friends, or send it to your own friend.

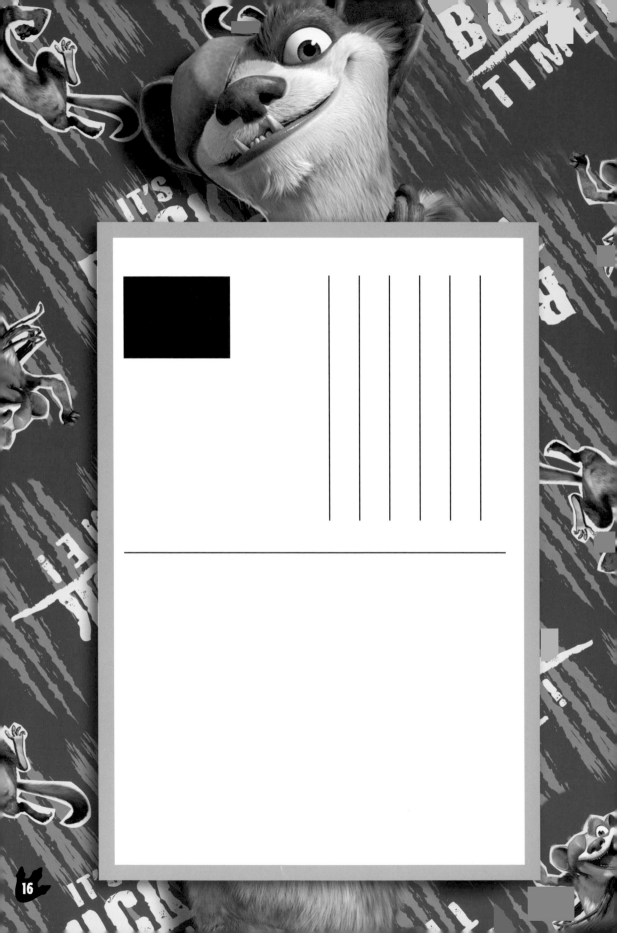

LEAVING THE HERD

One member of the herd isn't sure he will be welcome when Manny and Ellie have their baby. Cross out every letter below that appears twice, then unscramble the letters that are left to reveal who it is.

A D T R
T Y K
B Y V C G
E
K J V H J I
H R O C B A

The character is

_____

17

CRASH AND EDDIE FACT FILE

WHAT ARE THEY? Possums

PLACE IN THE HERD: Two brothers who are always getting into mischief.

LIKES: Adventure and their new friend Buck.

DISLIKES: Being sensible.

WHO IS IT?

Look carefully at the grid below.
Which character is above Manny, below Buck
and between Scrat and Crash?

Picture Puzzles

Fill in the missing characters in these two grids, by drawing a picture or writing their names. Each horizontal row should contain each image only once. Each vertical row should contain each image only once.

BUCK FACT FILE

WHAT IS HE?
A swashbuckling
one-eyed weasel.

LIVES: In the mysterious world of
the dinosaurs, beneath the Ice Age.

LIKES: Seeking revenge on Rudy, the
dinosaur who he had a fight with.

DISLIKES: The cold of the Ice Age.

22

MISSING LETTERS

Fill in the missing letter in each word,
to spell out the name of a character.

1. DI_GO
2. MOMMA _INO
3. RU_Y
4. S_D
5. _LLIE

The character is

_____

DiNOSAUr DRAWiNG

You will need:

Friends to play with
A piece of paper and a pen
or pencil for each player

1 Each player draws the
head of a dinosaur at the top
of their piece of
paper, without showing
it to anyone else.

2 Fold the top over so that
just the neck is showing.

3 Everyone passes their paper to the
person on their left.

4 Next draw the dinosaur's body, fold the paper over and pass it on again.

5 Continue in this way until each dinosaur has a tail, legs and feet.

6 Then unfold the pieces of paper and see what kind of scary
dinosaurs you have created!

BUCK'S I-SPY

Buck loves to play I-spy!
Play this game with one
or more friends.

1 Take turns looking around you
and choosing something that
you can both see.
Don't tell anyone what
it is.

2 Say "I spy with my
little eye, something
beginning with..." and give the
first letter of the name of the
object you can see.

3 The other players take
turns trying to guess what you
have seen.

4 Whoever correctly guesses the answer
takes the next turn.

MOMMA DINOSAUR FACT FILE

WHAT IS SHE? A fierce Tyrannosaurus Rex.
LIVES: Beneath the Ice Age in a land of dinosaurs.
LIKES: Her three babies.
DISLIKES: That her babies love Sid and don't want to eat him.

MANNY'S MOBILE

Make a mobile like Manny with the characters on this page and the next. Ask a grown-up to help you cut out the characters and make holes through the top of each one, by putting the adhesive putty or play dough under the picture and pushing the point of the pencil through it. Tie a piece of cotton to each one and tie them to the coat hanger to complete your mobile.

You will need:
Scissors
Cotton
A wire coat hanger
Sharp pencil
Adhesive putty or play dough

RUDY
Fact File

WHAT IS HE? An albino Baryonyx dinosaur.

LIVES: Down beneath the Ice Age in the land of the dinosaurs.

LIKES: Fighting Buck.

DISLIKES: That Buck uses his own tooth as a weapon against him.

Answers

PAGE 3 DIEGO'S RESCUE

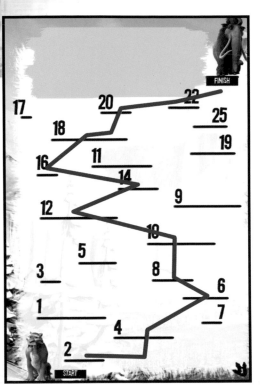

PAGE 11 HOW MANY MANNYS?
There are 9 Mannys.

PAGE 17 LEAVING THE HERD.
Diego thinks about leaving.

PAGE 19 WHO IS IT?
The answer is Sid.

PAGE 20 PICTURE PUZZLES

PAGE 23 MISSING LETTERS
The answer is Eddie.

PAGE 12 WHAT HAPPENED?
Diego and Sid felt left out because Manny and Ellie were going to have a baby. They were worried they would no longer be part of the herd. Diego left by himself. Sid found three dinosaur eggs and decided to keep them. But there was a problem: the dino babies' Momma came to find them, and took Sid with them to Lava Falls, in the land beneath the Ice Age where the other dinosaurs live.

The others followed to rescue him. On the way, they met Buck, an adventuring weasel, who helped them when they almost got eaten by strange plants and fierce dinosaurs. Buck was trying to find a dinosaur called Rudy, who he once had a fight with.

Eventually, they found Sid, who realised that the dino babies would be happier with the other dinosaurs, because they were now too big for him to look after. They made their way home, but not before Ellie had a baby called Peaches. Buck decided to stay in the dinosaur world, to continue his battle with Rudy.